SandCastle

Sight Words

Did You See One Jump?

Mary Elizabeth Salzmann

Consulting Editor Monica Marx, M.A./Reading Specialist

Published by SandCastle™, an imprint of ABDO Publishing Company, 4940 Viking Drive, Edina, Minnesota 55435.

Printed in the United States.

Credits
Edited by: Pam Price
Curriculum Coordinator: Nancy Tuminelly
Cover and Interior Design and Production: Mighty Media
Photo Credits: Comstock, Digital Vision, Eyewire Images, Image Source, ImageState, PhotoDisc, Stockbyte

Library of Congress Cataloging-in-Publication Data

Salzmann, Mary Elizabeth, 1968-
    Did you see one jump? / Mary Elizabeth Salzmann.
       p. cm. -- (Sight words)
    Includes index.
    Summary: Uses simple sentences, photographs, and a brief story to introduce six different words: can, come, did, or, to, very.
    ISBN 1-59197-466-6
    1. Readers (Primary) 2. Vocabulary--Juvenile literature. [1. Reading.] I. Title. II. Series.

PE1119.S2342157 2003
428.1--dc21

2003050310

SandCastle™ books are created by a professional team of educators, reading specialists, and content developers around five essential components that include phonemic awareness, phonics, vocabulary, text comprehension, and fluency. All books are written, reviewed, and leveled for guided reading, early intervention reading, and Accelerated Reader® programs and designed for use in shared, guided, and independent reading and writing activities to support a balanced approach to literacy instruction.

Let Us Know

After reading the book, SandCastle would like you to tell us your stories about reading. What is your favorite page? Was there something hard that you needed help with? Share the ups and downs of learning to read. We want to hear from you! To get posted on the ABDO Publishing Company Web site, send us e-mail at:

sandcastle@abdopub.com

SandCastle Level: Beginning

Featured Sight Words

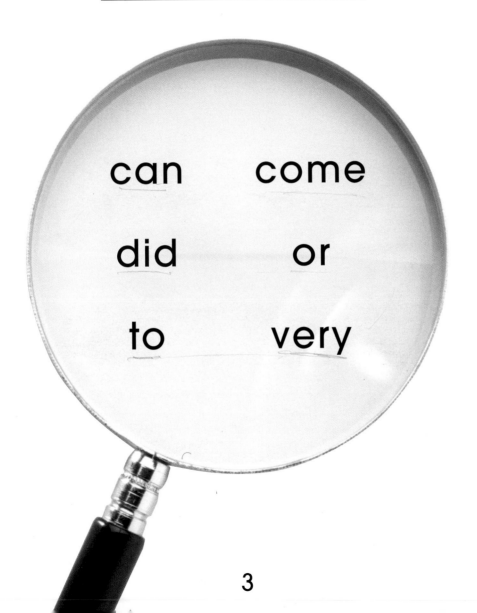

can come

did or

to very

Ray and Mike
can play the piano.

Ken and Dan wait for their mom to come.

Jenny's brother did
eat a banana.

Does Kate make her brother laugh or cry?

Ann and Gail read
to their brother.

Jordan's brother runs very fast.

Lance Goes Fishing

Lance, Kyle, and Fred are brothers.

Lance and his dad like to fish very much.

They can catch bass or trout.

Sometimes Fred and
Barky come too.

Lance asks Fred,
"Did you see one
jump?"

More Sight Words in This Book

a	make
and	much
are	one
eat	see
for	the
her	their
his	they
like	you

All words identified as sight words in this book are from
Edward Bernard Fry's "First Hundred Instant Sight Words."

Picture Index

banana, p. 9

cry, p. 11

dad, p. 18

mom, p. 7

piano, p. 5

read, p. 13

About SandCastle™

A professional team of educators, reading specialists, and content developers created the SandCastle™ series to support young readers as they develop reading skills and strategies and increase their general knowledge. The SandCastle™ series has four levels that correspond to early literacy development in young children. The levels are provided to help teachers and parents select the appropriate books for young readers.

Emerging Readers
(no flags)

Beginning Readers
(1 flag)

Transitional Readers
(2 flags)

Fluent Readers
(3 flags)

These levels are meant only as a guide. All levels are subject to change.

To see a complete list of SandCastle™ books and other nonfiction titles from ABDO Publishing Company, visit www.abdopub.com or contact us at:

4940 Viking Drive, Edina, Minnesota 55435 • 1-800-800-1312 • fax: 1-952-831-1632